EDGE
BOOKS™

✦INTO THE GREAT OUTDOORS✦

# TURKEY HUNTING
## For Kids

BY TYLER OMOTH

Consultant:
Greg Slone
Next Generation Hunting
Bowling Green, Kentucky

CAPSTONE PRESS
a capstone imprint

Edge Books are published by Capstone Press,
1710 Roe Crest Drive, North Mankato, Minnesota 56003.
www.capstonepub.com

*Library of Congress Cataloging-in-Publication Data*
Omoth, Tyler.
  Turkey hunting for kids / by Tyler Omoth.
    p. cm.—(Edge books. into the great outdoors)
  Includes bibliographical references and index.
  Summary: "Explores the sport of turkey hunting, including its rich history,
specific gear, special techniques, safety requirements, and conservation
efforts"—Provided by publisher.
  ISBN 978-1-4296-8615-0 (library binding)
  ISBN 978-1-4296-9270-0 (paperback)
  ISBN 978-1-62065-228-2 (ebook PDF)
  1. Turkey hunting—Juvenile literature. I. Title.
SK325.T8O66 2013
799.2′4645—dc23                                    2011051836

**Editorial Credits**
Christopher L. Harbo, editor; Ted Williams, designer; Marcie Spence,
    media researcher; Sarah Schuette, photo stylist; Marcy Morin,
    scheduler; Laura Manthe, production specialist

**Photo Credits**
Alamy: North Wind Picture Archives, 6 (top); Capstone Studio: Karon
Dubke, 10–11, 24, 25; Corbis: John E Marriott/All Canada Photos, 9;
Dwight Kuhn Photography: David Kuhn, 18; iStockphoto: BirdImages,
cover, JEVader, 6-7, JohnHuelskamp, 13; Newscom: ZUMA Press, 15,
28–29; Shutterstock: andersphoto, design element, Bruce MacQueen, 1, 26,
Bryan Eastham, 4–5, 22, Chris Turner, 3, 19, Dewayne Flowers, 14, Edvard
Molnar, design element, Gerald A. DeBoer, 16, HomeStudio, design
element, Jeff Banke, 21, Sebastian Knight, design element, Sergii Figurnyi,
design element

Printed in the United States of America in Stevens Point, Wisconsin.
032012      006678WZF12

# TABLE OF CONTENTS

# CHAPTER 1

# PRIZE GOBBLER

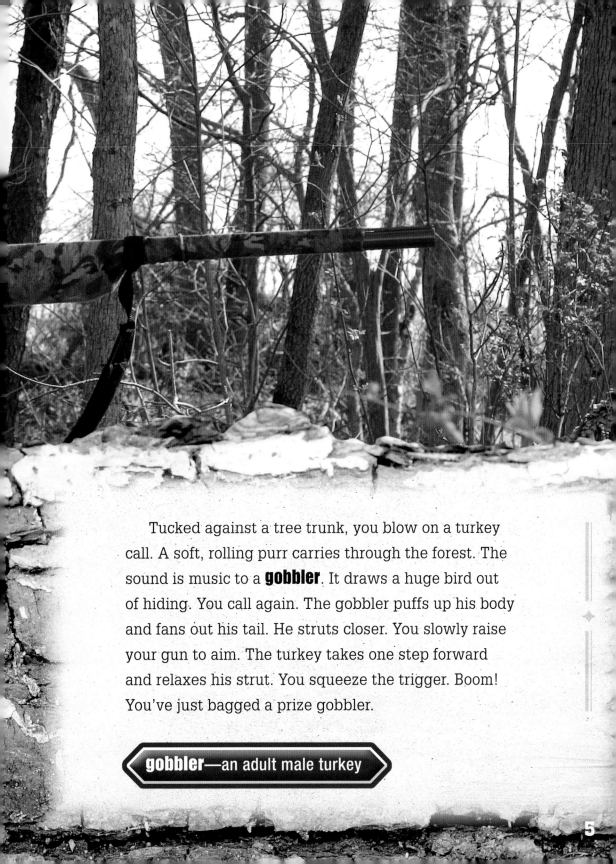

Tucked against a tree trunk, you blow on a turkey call. A soft, rolling purr carries through the forest. The sound is music to a **gobbler**. It draws a huge bird out of hiding. You call again. The gobbler puffs up his body and fans out his tail. He struts closer. You slowly raise your gun to aim. The turkey takes one step forward and relaxes his strut. You squeeze the trigger. Boom! You've just bagged a prize gobbler.

**gobbler**—an adult male turkey

# History

Turkey hunting has a long history in North America. About 4,000 years ago, American Indians made turkey calls to draw birds in for a kill. Turkey feathers decorated their clothing. About 10 million turkeys lived throughout North America. When the Europeans arrived in the 1500s, turkeys were a plentiful food source.

## FACT

Benjamin Franklin wanted the wild turkey to be the United States' national bird. He said the turkey was a "bird of courage."

But overhunting soon hurt wild turkey populations. In the mid-1700s, hunters sold turkey meat at markets. Market hunting wiped out turkeys in nearly half of their original **habitats**. By the late 1920s, less than 30,000 wild turkeys roamed the United States.

In 1937 lawmakers passed the Federal Aid in Wildlife Restoration Act. This act taxed ammunition, guns, and other hunting equipment. Some of the money received from the act was used to boost the turkey population. Today more than 7 million wild turkeys live in North America.

**habitat**—the natural place and conditions in which an animal or plant lives

## Species

Wild turkeys are divided into just two **species**, the Ocellated turkey and the North American wild turkey. The Ocellated turkey makes its home in southern Mexico and Central America.

The North American wild turkey is broken into five subspecies. The eastern wild turkey is the most common subspecies in the United States. Its range mainly stretches from the East Coast to Minnesota. In the western Great Plains, hunters stalk the Rio Grande turkey. The Rio Grande is the smallest North American turkey and has tan-tipped feathers on its tail. The Merriam's wild turkey enjoys wooded areas like those in the Rocky Mountains. The Osceola turkey has a limited range. It lives almost entirely in Florida. The Gould's wild turkey is the largest and the least common in the United States. It struts in Arizona and New Mexico.

**species**—a group of plants or animals that share common characteristics

**Turkey Range Map**

Eastern
Gould's
Merriam's
Ocellated
Osceola
Rio Grande

Merriam's wild turkey

# CHAPTER 2

# HUNTING GEAR

Turkey hunters need the right equipment to get the job done. The right gun or bow is key to making the perfect shot. Turkey calls can lure the birds in closer. **Camouflage** clothing and gear hides you from the turkey's keen eyesight.

## Guns and Bows

Most turkey hunters use shotguns. For young hunters, a 20-gauge shotgun is easy to carry and aim. It provides enough firepower to take down a turkey without a lot of **recoil**. When using a 20-gauge, wait until the turkey is within 30 yards (27 meters) before taking the shot. Adult hunters usually use a 12-gauge shotgun. A 12-gauge has more firepower and a longer range.

Choosing the right ammunition is as important as picking the right gun. Shotguns use shells filled with small pellets called shot. The best shot sizes for turkey hunting are 4, 5, and 6.

**camouflage**—coloring or covering that makes animals, people, and objects look like their surroundings

**recoil**—the kickback of a gun when firing

Some turkey hunters enjoy the extra challenge of bowhunting. When choosing a bow, consider its draw length and draw weight. The draw length is how far back you have to pull the bowstring. The draw weight is the amount of effort it takes to draw the bowstring back. Try out several bows and pick one that feels the most comfortable to you. For turkey hunting, use broadhead arrows. They allow you to bring down a large bird quickly and cleanly.

## Turkey Calls

Turkey hunters usually use **friction** calls and air calls to draw in birds. Friction calls are used by rubbing or striking two objects together to make turkey sounds. Slate pot calls are a very popular friction call. By striking a rod on a small stone disc, these calls can make realistic turkey yelps, clucks, and purrs.

Air calls let hunters make turkey noises by blowing through reeds. These calls are small and easy to carry. But air calls take a lot of practice to master. Buy your air call early so you can practice before hunting season.

**friction**—a force produced when two objects rub together

slate pot call

## CALLING FOR THE SEASONS

Spring turkey hunting is focused on gobblers. The best calls to use to lure them close are the yelp, putt, and purr of a hen or the gobble of another male. In the fall the birds are trying to stay together. Calls that imitate a lost bird work best. The "kee-kee-kee" of a young lost turkey and the plain cluck are good choices for fall hunting.

# Camouflage

Turkeys have amazing eyesight. To stay hidden, turkey hunters wear camouflage from head to toe. Camouflage boots, pants, shirts, jackets, and even face masks help you blend into the woods. Be sure to think about where you will be hunting before choosing your camouflage. If you are hunting among leafy trees, pick a camouflage pattern that matches. Choose green or brown camouflage depending on the time of year you are hunting.

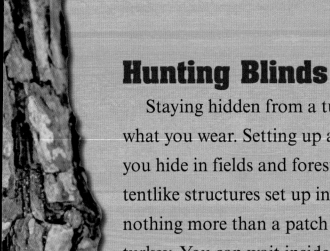

# Hunting Blinds

Staying hidden from a turkey isn't just about what you wear. Setting up a hunting blind can help you hide in fields and forests. These camouflaged tentlike structures set up in minutes. They look like nothing more than a patch of trees or bushes to a turkey. You can wait inside and keep an eye out for approaching birds from any direction.

# CHAPTER 3

# TIPS AND TECHNIQUES

## FACT

In the United States, people can hunt turkeys in every state but Alaska.

Bringing down a turkey is a thrill. But you must know when and where to hunt to be successful. You also need to know where to aim to bag a trophy bird.

## Seasons

Spring and fall are the two main turkey hunting seasons. Nearly every state has a spring season. Spring turkey hunting allows hunters to take gobblers while the females are preparing to nest. The gobblers' desire to mate makes them eager to respond to hen calls.

The rules are different for fall hunting. Both male and female turkeys can be hunted in most states in the fall. During autumn, turkeys like to stay in flocks. Drawing them into firing range can be difficult. One fall hunting tactic is to startle the flock. This tactic involves putting your gun down and running and yelling at the flock. After the birds scatter, you hide near the place where the flock first gathered. Then you use calls that sound like a lost bird to draw turkeys back in for a shot.

# Where to Hunt

Turkeys thrive in many habitats, including forests, swamps, and deserts. When you scout, look for the resources turkeys need most. Like all animals, turkeys need food and water. Streams, ponds, and lakes can provide the drinking water flocks need. When it comes to food, turkeys are not picky eaters. They'll eat insects, nuts, berries, and grains. Acorns are a particular favorite of turkeys. Look for areas that have these foods, and check the ground for claw scratches. If turkeys have looked for food there before, they'll likely come back.

Turkeys often look for food and mates in open, grassy areas near trees and shrubs. In these areas, look for shallow bowl-shaped marks in loose or sandy soil. These marks are dusting bowls. Dusting is a turkey's way of taking a bath. These dusting bowls are usually visited often.

**FACT**
Turkeys can run 25 miles (40 kilometers) per hour. That's faster than most Olympic sprinters.

# Where to Aim

Every turkey hunter wants to make a clean kill. Where you aim depends on whether you are hunting with a shotgun or a bow.

When shotgun hunting, aim for the turkey's head and neck. Since birdshot may not drive deep into the body, aiming for the head and neck is the easiest way to make a clean kill. But before you shoot, wait for the right moment. While a turkey struts, it pulls its head in toward its body. This movement makes for a tough shot. Wait for the turkey to relax and extend its neck away from its body before shooting.

Bowhunting uses a different approach. The bird's head is too small of a target for a bow and arrow. Aim for the vital **organs** of the body instead. Target the area near where the turkey's wing meets the body. An arrow that drives deep into this area will puncture the heart or lungs and score a clean kill.

**organ**—a part of the body that does a certain job; the heart, lungs, and kidneys are organs

# THE DOMINANT GOBBLER

To bag the biggest bird, you must spot the **dominant** gobbler. Fortunately, the signs are easy to pick out. First look for the largest gobbler with the longest beard. He is likely to be the dominant male. The dominant bird will also strut the most. Finally, if one male turkey always chases away other males, he is likely the dominant gobbler.

**dominant**—the most powerful or important

firearm target

bow hunting target

# CHAPTER 4

# SAFETY

While turkey hunting is a fun sport, it does have some risks. Every hunter should keep safety in mind at all times.

## General Safety

All hunters should follow a few basic safety precautions every time they hunt. Before you set out, tell someone where you plan to hunt and how long you will be out. Also, pack a basic survival kit. It can include a cell phone, water, rope, first-aid supplies, a knife, and a waterproof fire-starting kit.

## The Right Spot

One of the most important turkey hunting safety rules is to find a safe hunting spot. Find a location that faces an open area. From this spot you should have a good view of the clearing and be able to see other hunters as well. Next find a tree that is wide enough to cover your entire back and lean up against it. If other hunters are in the area, the tree will protect you from being hit by stray shots.

# Gun and Bow Safety

Any time you carry a gun or a bow, safety comes first. Guns should always be completely unloaded before entering a vehicle, house, or camp. You should always keep the gun's **safety** in the "on" position until you are ready to fire at a target. Before firing, be certain of your target and make sure no one is standing behind it.

**safety**—a device that prevents a gun from firing

**FACT**
Never let red, white, or blue colors peek out from underneath your camouflage. These colors can be mistaken for a gobbler's head.

quiver

Bowhunters also need to follow some simple safety rules. Walking through trees and brush increases your risk of tripping and falling. Always keep arrows safely stored in a **quiver** while walking to your hunting spot. Only nock an arrow in your bow when you have a turkey in sight and you are ready to shoot. As with guns, be sure no other hunters are in your line of fire before you release an arrow.

**quiver**—a container for arrows

25

Nearly 3 million people enjoy turkey hunting in the United States. To keep the sport strong for the future, hunters must do their part to **conserve** turkey populations and habitats. Obeying hunting rules and joining conservation organizations are two ways to help the sport.

# Hunting Conservation

One of the best ways to protect the turkey population is to practice responsible hunting habits. Hunters should only shoot birds that are allowed by their license. State hunting regulations are set to keep the turkey population healthy. Each state has its own rules and regulations. Hunters should learn and follow the laws wherever they hunt.

It's also important to wait for a good shot and take the bird cleanly. Taking a shot that is out of range or too close to other turkeys can lead to injured birds.

**conserve**—to save

# Organizations

Hunting and conservation organizations have done a lot to restore turkey populations in the United States. The National Wild Turkey Federation (NWTF) raises money to help protect wild turkey habitats. The organization also supports responsible turkey hunting by educating new hunters.

You can get involved with many state and local organizations. Check with your state's department of natural resources. Some states offer classes and programs to learn more about hunting, conservation, and nature.

The fun and excitement of turkey hunting has been enjoyed by generations of hunters. With proper conservation, the thrill of bagging these amazing birds will be possible for new generations of hunters too.

# GLOSSARY

**camouflage** (KA-muh-flahzh)—coloring or covering that makes animals, people, and objects look like their surroundings

**conserve** (kuhn-SURV)—to save

**dominant** (DOM-uh-nuhnt)—the most powerful or important

**friction** (FRIK-shuhn)—a force produced when two objects rub together

**gobbler** (GOB-luhr)—an adult male turkey

**habitat** (HAB-uh-tat)—the natural place and conditions in which an animal or plant lives

**organ** (OR-guhn)—a part of the body that does a certain job; the heart, lungs, and kidneys are organs

**quiver** (KWIV-ur)—a container for arrows

**recoil** (RI-koil)—the kickback of a gun when firing

**safety** (SAYF-tee)—a device that prevents a gun from firing

**species** (SPEE-sheez)—a group of plants or animals that share common characteristics

# READ MORE

**Canino, Kate.** *Turkey Hunting.* Hunting: Pursuing Wild Game! New York: Rosen Pub.'s Rosen Central, 2011.

**Gunderson, Jessica.** *Bowhunting for Fun!* For Fun! Minneapolis: Compass Point Books, 2009.

**MacRae, Sloan.** *Turkey Hunting.* Open Season. New York: PowerKids Press, 2011.

# INTERNET SITES

FactHound offers a safe, fun way to find Internet sites related to this book. All of the sites on FactHound have been researched by our staff.

Here's all you do:

Visit *www.facthound.com*

Type in this code: 9781429686150

 Check out projects, games and lots more at **www.capstonekids.com**

# INDEX